THEY
WORSE WHEN
THEY'RE WET.

Molly Jackson

THEY LOOK WORSE WHEN THEY'RE WET. © 2022 Molly Jackson

All rights reserved.

Presentation by *BookLeaf Publishing*

Web: www.bookleafpub.com

E-mail: info@bookleafpub.com

ISBN: 9789395621168

First edition 2022

The Serving Hatch

Every evening,
at 7pm, we open the serving hatch.

We take it in turns to put something behind the
hatch doors, but I always open them.
Opposite the closed hatch is the dining table,
where he sits while I open it; he's supposed to
look at the hatch from there, but often I must
wait a while after

7pm for him to be paying attention.
Tonight, I open the hatch. It was his turn to put
something behind it--- my hair...
This synthetic black hair slicked into thick black
leech strands.
Put me in water.

Sometimes I assume these objects are passive
aggressive
like mine sometimes are. The teeth and legs fall
out,
the fingers poke through.

There have been times when I haven't even
opened the doors to the hatch because I know
I'm going to be disappointed. What's worse are

the times when I have opened the doors and
known nothing was going to be there.

Stir

This pan was perfect,
the creamiest thing I had seen and so smooth; I
hated it.
Standing back,
brimming, I said in my head: 'I desperately want
to knock that pan off the edge',
I wondered if I was joking. These are the things
I don't say out loud, because they
ruin.
'I desperately want to knock that pan off the
edge', my tone cheeky but honest,
loud enough, like I wanted it to be.
After a few minutes
of deftly chopping up my own questions about
what I had said,
nothing else coming from outside to interrupt
the echo impression
my faultless, playful, lightly cutting sentence,
I started to wonder if I had even said anything at
all.
Pitch black.
Sea. Bed.
Causal.
The floppy idiot impression,
slapped around. And we went to bed;

it's still slopping around my head.

The morning: a skin had formed over the white slick.

Two Times

They were earthy and fine.
A while later Guy Fawkes appeared on the wall,
and it was hard to laugh.
Then I laughed so hard my face thought it was
sobbing,
then it was.

A treat or treating,
mutually, we disappeared.
All of a sudden
Unbearable
Oh my animals…

meeting

They look at me in my chair, I stand up, say my
name, and
"I'm 22 years old and I've been quiet for 60
years".
The oldest lady lets out a worried gasp,
And it reminds me of when the receptionist at
the doctors did the same thing,
when I went to make an appointment about the
lump in my throat.

Success

How do you answer closed questions?
YES…   MMM
if it can be leisurely.
The roughest wall my knuckles have seen yet. I
tuck them into my sleeve.
I'll do it all the time, I'd do it all the time.
I could be thinking about you, or the bricks.

Little little
How does it go when home? How does it go
home, everyone here?

We all nervously put our half full glasses of
sparkling water on the windowsill.
Crunchy, compressed for the picture, standing
closely together, hot.

All at the same time,
We realise no one will know whose glass is
whose.
The shutter might have clicked, but no one could
have heard it
for the prickly fizz of those waters.

Needless to say,
the picture came out terribly.

Scape

In the dark, the evening, he brought round
animals we could shoot:
some sheep, goats, guinea pigs.
I went around to the other side of the barn; I
didn't want to see.
Please kill them properly, please kill them,
please kill them.
The shots and the bleating. The animals jumping
out from the other side of the barn, a human
queue with long thin guns, barn divider, wounds
and fear on the other side.
Wooden or otherwise, dark can't know.
A large sheep had been shot and was bleeding
out black bleeding.
On the other side.
Its lamb ambled over, and it was being shot at
too. Tiny oblivious head, maybe. I looked into
the sheep's balled eyes and raised my little
finger to a human. A promise of continuation,
I gave it. I'm fucking disgusting.
A small goat hurled through the air from the left.
This is so much pain.
I dribbled and looked at the edge of my mug
where my mouth had been. Waxy pink marks. I
hit disgust thinking about what kind of crayony

shit they had been doing to my mug, then fell into my heart. My mum used this yesterday, and this is her lipstick.

I would rather die than see all of this. I would rather die than see all of this.

One Time a Day

Tired of being the one that's infantile.
Ruffles my
hair ends, what's this? It's darker… Is it darker
now? It hasn't been much time, longer.
Will you clear the table. Hello, say hello.
(chair to foot end, wincing, small, excruciating,
pain overlap, hot embarrassing, excruciating,
pain increasing and, resisting, forgiving, then
inflection).
Waiting for someone to ask, wait for the
question about. Someone ask why I'm crying.
and
even then, see chance waning, nervous,
humiliated to say, that the chair is on my seven
year old toes, and it has been for some time.
I'm sorry, I am sorry—too shy to say it.
Dent grey school shoe; little strap. Fuzzed
velcro,
tiny purple toenail.
Longer now. Curled hair ends, darker more.
Imagine the
blood, those
small, crumpled
shoe ends. Minor, concave, crushed-in leather
toe. Guilty little heart, darker hair now.

Black-purple little nail.
No blood. I have poked myself in the eye, guilty
blanket. The heavy girl's chair is on my toes.
Seep, how to do it? How does it go when the
lights are off? Little blood edge,
brown purple, seven years old. To black hair
ends of my twenty two years old.
How do you change? How does it go when the
lights are off?
Hot eyes, little prawn eyes. She salts my
bathwater; I make starch from my body.
Slick little prawn eyes, salt crust. Purple toenail,
bright white shell half against it, compressed.
Chair release. How do you change the ashamed
tiny heart beads, rattle out the chest, the
mortified little heart in there. What does it do
when the lights are off? Those tiny white heart
beads, tiny rattle, hole in each, pearly shamed,
shamed. Inverted bottled, shamed, pearly rattle.
Salted water; I have wanted to swim.

Stop tap

Voice like the leg of an
Uneven table. Legs cut
Wrongly, unlevelled,
Unlevelled and voiced
Wrong.
Wrongly.
I'll assume
Oh, angry? We were angry?

Down to the quick,
Pulsey.
Sick.
Cheesy nail.
Socks gone wrong, stroke gentle rib
Back rib, soothe.

Turn everything off
If you want me to talk
Talking to hear me
Turn off this tap,
I can't speak over it. Tap more expressive than
my opinion on how this day is going
Or the hot
The tap's SHHHFFFFHSHSHHHH is more
expressive than anyone
In this place.

Life's Mission

We've had this plan in place for a very long time. Years of planning has led up to this, a lot matters, a lot is riding on this.

In the last few months, we have been intensely working with tens of specialists: neurologists, IT, philosophers, more, for this day. We are now watching intently; this is crucial innovative research.

We have set up the presentation so that you cannot change the slide by yourself.

We're going to sit mutely behind our letters watching your eyes change as you at first notice that there might be a problem—the initial hope, you click again. This shifts into confusion, 'oh, the slide isn't changing', you say.

We meet this with our stony initials.

Maybe some frustration or anxiety is beginning to occur now: 'is it my device? Has the slide changed for everyone else?'

you inquire desperately.

This is a delicate operation. We fretfully look at each other, we pray no one will be stupidly overcome by empathy and type in the chat that

the slide hasn't changed. For this, you have to feel alone
and unreal.
No one does it. Perhaps you pretend to be amused.
It has been about fifteen seconds now. We watch you fluster and sweat and struggle.
'HAHA BLOODY TECHNOLOGY',
you grasp at humour and first world relatability for salvation. By now you're either really pissed off or scared.
We are waiting for a signal that's incredibly tight and specific; a tiny careful decision will be made soon.
Your voice starts to shake and weaken… we change the slide.

Jesus

worse than the pain of not being able to
close my hand
worse than the pain of not being able to
shut my hand
splinter
worse than not being able to hold a
needle comfortably between my lips
worse than it rolling on the
floor.
I know it's only [this shop]
the problem is it's any shop.
worse than not being able to squeeze
either side.
a needle is so close to being exactly what I
need.

Light Pink Fabric

After, I looked down at the arms, two next to
each other. My arm looked like a man's arm.
This means I have become responsible and
rough. Tough now.
This morning, walking through the school kids,
I heard a boy ask his mum if an aeroplane has
ever crashed.
She paused and said yes,
and he asked when.
We can tell children anything...
I hoped about the severity of the example she
gave.
I'm sighing about things;
when I arrived home, I put pins in two. Felt
present moment, written in biro, and the meat of
my thumb pad. Because
While I was being vain upstairs, my mother
became very sad.
The things I want
The things we want
We're all gritting our teeth so hard that the bile
rises from our stomach to the under jaw...
You never embarrass me.

Out Out

It was silent for a while, as I expected,
But a little time after leaving the house, looking
out the window, its seatbelt deep in its fur.
it said that -by leaving that house-
it felt like it had survived some kind of
extraordinary disaster

whether natural or not…
now it was free
or felt rescued
but
it said really fucking quietly

now I see too much

It stamped on the green tomatoes it had spent
Months being excited for. It sat on the concrete
Patio. The insects blurred.
We smell their smoke. Tears run down its
muzzle face, roundy.
Slowly, so linear and polite, like woodlice.
He stands meters away, sighing, hands on hips.
It's mentally ill he says over the fence. In the
same way you'd

Say 'he's a prick'. Like the bite marks on my
arm
Aren't burning and my tomatoes aren't crushed.
Wilted spinach slides my fingers across
Wrist. That spill won't ever come off. The
deposit,
£300, is the amount I would pay to have it shot
In the head
Eyes closed white yellow red
And still won't say something here has finished.

Treasure

So well and not at all. Give it to me. I don't say
it to be dramatic.

'non-plussed' by my
I don't expect anyone to hear me
Duvet against the table sounds like it. I have
flipped my mug shaking the duvet, anyway
Lots of flies… LOTS of flies

How the HELL

Encounter with Idiot with Loud Motorbike

I sincerely introduce myself as Reality; my legs
are shaking.
"your guts are rotten" but it comes out as "your
rots are gutten". "your rots are gutten and so is
your sodding bike. You Pillock". he stabs me
a few times in the chest and I walk off.
Get that thing where I need to scream and it fills
my mouth, but do something with shoulders
instead.
Somewhere else, two long boys in black outfits
Walk into the shop and they come out with
sweets.

When I get home, I'm still not satisfied.
There's something I desperately need and I don't
Know what it is
I used to think it was romance
Then I thought it was any kind of hug or
physical violence
Then alone time
And I, I have had everything I thought.
Think the problem is

I need my wisdom teeth

I want to be teething.

The stab wounds are just stupid clots, I'll be fine

Cash

I washed two
Thousand glass jars
Threw them into a bag
And the sound of them crashing together
One at a time
Happily destroyed my hearing

Different Creams

The second it started
Raining
I got exactly what I wanted
Cold spitty peace
The clip of the toe, the click of the dry heel

Oh no, sounds
Like a kitten

Everything in my pocket,
had stopped paying attention to me.
I learned that to rough
Is a verb.
My elephant skin fingers,
Dear,
Deer,
We might have been
Roughed

Pressing the Corners

Today behind the small doors: Dark Brown
Teddy
Quite big
with "PLEASE KNEEL" written on a ribbon
that leads
from a white wide loop around his neck onto his
hay-filled tummy-chest, stomach? Middle mass.
Embroidered please kneel, prayer mat.
I have three to offer—"I Know, It's Okay,
Sorry".
and it's finished, as easy as the three

Forked silky endings, a bit frayed.
Rock hard nose plastic, I remember it hitting my
front two teeth and forehead. Or hitting my teeth
through my top lip.
Semi-attractive red lip sore where it.

It has picked up damp from those big flags
Cold stone church, mouldy straw inside. Dry
outer layers, blue-grey dust.
Wet cold guts centre.

Earth Work

I had felt confidence growing on my pip when I
was in London. Little scraps of red
orange slimy flesh reforming
and sewing together on the seed. When I got
back, brave with decisions,
I saw a caterpillar on my leg at the desk and
brushed it off; it disappeared under a cabinet so
Now It Will Die In An Office.
One of those times where something is
magically gone.
I have tried to feed it my flesh confidence, now I
hate myself,
and it's going to die anyway. The pip
is mostly dried, died. I'm imagining
a small, embossed silver box that I will collect
the caterpillar in tomorrow
when I'm there,
but I don't have a box like that. The caterpillar
will
crisp up on the office carpet, where no one will
see it until the work
moves somewhere else,
or there's a flood.

Cages

I rubbed my eyes until I saw new kinds of purple
And I saw the giraffe I wanted to sew.
I rubbed my eyes until my wrists ached.
The phone rang: no,
I still haven't managed it.
Outside, I breathed
With the elderly.
I sat on a bench with them and,
As she spoke
I felt her lungs rattling the bench's back.
Those old lungs.
And I looked at my lap.
Through her 1950s fashion
In the photo album,
While her lungs rattled my back,
And her lungs rattled my lungs.
The same as a lot of ice in a paper cup,
Or the crunch of bass.

Doors Are Heavy

Doors are heavy.

Last Note

Made eye contact with a tall man driving a
small car. Doing the same. His shirt said he was
ashamed,
But hope not

Now a teenager, living at home, without
Teenage confidence, too old, and too shy.
and my body

a mild breed of communication that
won't tolerate
why should I care if you float, like you're in the
sea?

Haven't got excuses;
The legs come off and she'll get the bus
nothing makes it past the threshold

Yes and yes and yes and yes
there are always ways
not stop to me

Ingram Content Group UK Ltd.
Milton Keynes UK
UKHW022014130423
420127UK00015B/1472